# ECFMG-Certified:
## Career Options for the International Medical Graduate

OLAREWAJU OLADIPO, MD MBA

# FOREWORD

This book complements the books previously written on the subject of international medical graduate education. The motivation for writing this book stems from my experience in mentoring international medical graduates who after passing the required qualifying examinations – USMLE, to begin post-graduate residency training in the United States struggle to secure a position to embark on this important phase in their career. The reason for this predicament is simple – there are just not enough positions for every international graduates that apply for the available limited training positions, that is, whatever is left after participating US medical graduates are 'matched'. The frustration faced by this select group is real, with many becoming disillusioned having left their countries of origin, and devoted countless hours and limited financial resources in pursuit of their dreams – a dream to practice and earn a living as a physician in the United States.

This book, just like the other ones on the subject of international medical graduate education series is geared towards this small, but significant group of international medical graduates with aspirations to pursue a career in the United States.

The objective of this book is to educate those who in the profession, who for one reason, or the other are facing difficulties in moving forward, and are unable to secure opportunities to enter into a residency training program. The primary goal is to provoke the thought among international medical graduates in such predicaments to consider the many other career options that exist outside of the realm of clinical practice of medicine. The options are actually many, for those who dare to look. As someone whose career has spanned multiple fields, in and outside of the clinical practice of medicine, I truly believe it is possible to enjoy a fulfilling career in the United States, even when the door to undergo residency training is closed.

Embarking on a career outside of the clinical practice of medicine is not always a preferred path for many international medical graduates, especially in the immediate period after arriving in the United States. In many cases, such a decision is the outcome of uncontrollable circumstances, often the result of lost opportunities to enter into a residency training program. My primary goal in writing this book is to enlighten international medical graduates on the reality of entering into a residency training program, but in addition to adequately preparing them to enter into such training, to prepare them for one, or more alternative career paths. It is in the active consideration of this thought that one can not only improve their overall chances, but also prepare them to better handle the storm in the event that they are unable to secure a position to begin residency training.

As with the other books written on the subject of post-graduate medical education for the international medical, I strongly believe that the wisdom of this book is applicable to anyone in the profession who is keen to learn about alternative options. While this book is invaluable to international medical graduates who are having difficulties in making a headway in joining a residency program, it is useful to anyone in the profession, irrespective of the stage of their career - as a tool to enlighten the individual. In the pages that follow, career alternatives related to the field of medicine and in non-medical fields are discussed. While every effort has been made to identify specific, alternative career paths,  it is not the intention of this book to prescribe any particular option. Rather, it is my intention to stimulate your imagination such that you can see the possibilities out there, to be less constrained in your outlook, and to recognize the worth of their MD degree and your ECFMG certificate (for those who have successfully completed the required qualifying examination). This renewed approach to your professional life is bound to bring with it a sense of freedom and optimism, especially during those moments when one is faced with career challenges.

In the pages that follow, I have compiled a mix of career alternatives, some closely related to the practice of medicine, and others that are not so related to the medical field. I sincerely hope that in the process of reading this book, you will unlock hidden potentials that can further enrich your personal life.

# INTRODUCTION

It is a recognized fact that many of the international medical graduates that immigrate to the United States are a highly motivated group of individuals, with many in the top tier of their graduating class. It is this level of motivation to excel that led them to seek opportunities for career advancement and to pursue training opportunities in the United States. They see such opportunities as a natural progression in their professional journey. While many are filled with the ambition to pursue their dreams, many are ill-prepared to cope with the challenges that lie along the way.

In our ongoing work in mentoring international medical graduates at KAINJI, the primary emphasis continues to be on building a nurturing and a supporting network that equips applicants with the tools to excel in the United States Medical Licensing Examinations (USMLE) and become competitive applicants for residency training programs. Through this organization, and the effort of several other selfless individuals, many international medical graduates have attained success and have gained entry into competitive residency training programs in the United States.

Every year that the Match result is announced, while one shares the joy of those who are successful, one question repeatedly plays on my mind is – what happens to those left behind? The number of those left behind seem to get bigger as the years go  by, making the case to address the needs of this group. The main challenge is that there are not enough openings for residency training for every great candidate that applies for such a position. The steady yearly influx of international medical graduates from different countries into the United States, all in pursuit of the same goal, means that every year, a significant number will not get into residency programs. With such a reality in mind, additional effort is currently geared towards catering to the demands of the candidates who are unsuccessful in the Match. It is thus very important that such individuals are provided with the tools to guide them through the less familiar paths, and point them towards other opportunities to build a successful career outside of the practice of clinical medicine while at the same time guided to make the most of their medical diploma, and for those who qualify, their ECFMG certificate.

In my experience over the years working with international medical graduates, the thought of a career outside of direct patient care in clinical medicine is not readily entertained, or seen as a viable alternative. This sentiment is very understandable since many international medical graduates, especially the group that I am familiar with come from cultures that place great emphasis on utilizing one's medical education in the direct service of the sick. Among this group of international medical graduates, the thought of an alternative career is not usually considered as a primary intention, but only after they become overwhelmed and become disillusioned by repeated disappointments in their professional journey. It is during such moments of frustration and despair that many are prone to make poor career decisions, or settle for mediocre professional alternatives.

In addressing this challenge, our advisory team at KAINJI now advise applicants to consider the various career alternatives early in the process of preparing for the qualifying examinations - USMLE. This conversation is regularly held with every candidate, even the most competitive of all. It is our belief that such an approach, especially when dispensed early in the preparatory process has a dual advantage. It serves as a catalyst to prompt many to prepare for the worst-case scenario and think early of comparable career alternatives. This approach has also become a source of motivation to many, who then put in the extra effort and prepare well for the qualifying examination – USMLE. While some candidates hate to have the conversation, and see it as a distraction, it is recommended to everyone that seek our counsel. It is my belief that this approach to the issue at hand can be safely implemented while the candidates continue to pour their hearts and souls towards the primary goal of securing a residency training position in the United States.

# ECFMG-Certified: Career Options for the International Medical Graduate

The thought of an alternative career option can be a useful stimulus, one that forces an individual to take a critical look at what career choice aligns the most with his, or her inner desires. It encourages an individual to think deep about what other career alternatives out there is likely to offer a level of satisfaction that will match what he or she is likely to obtain from the practice of clinical medicine. While having such a candid conversation is not readily received by some applicants, it has led others, especially international medical graduates who have been out of medical school for some years – more than ten years, to make a decision that they have already considered but are unsure of how to go about it. For those graduates who have been out of medical school for ten years or more, the decision is generally easier to make, their reasoning being, rather than devote two to three years  to prepare for the qualifying examinations – USMLE and in the pursuit of the unlikely dream of securing a residency training position, they would rather pursue an alternative career option from the outset.

In instances when an individual choose not to sit the qualifying examinations - USMLE, they automatically forfeit the added opportunity that becoming ECFMG-certified confers. The drawback of this route is that such candidates may have to forgo some opportunities in field related to the practice of medicine, especially ones where having an ECFMG certificate is considered an asset. Such opportunities may be in areas like pharmaceutical research, clinical and non-clinical fellowships, and positions related to the field of clinical trials. Rather than have the applicant select an alternative career option at the outset, what matters most in this exercise is to challenge every applicant to at least give the subject a thought. In thinking about it, they get to explore their innermost desires and begin to seek knowledge of their interests and see it would serve them well as an alternative career choice.

It is not uncommon that some applicants refuse to entertain the thought of an alternative career. In my experience, I have found such candidates to be less prepared to cope with disappointments, and become overwhelmed when things fail to go according to plan. For such candidates, many of who are in the early stages of their career, the experience can leave them with a dent in their personal confidence and self-esteem. In my opinion, not to consider an alternative career option early enough is not a particularly wise decision. Rather than see the thought of considering an alternative career option as a *'Plan B'*, I advise that individuals see it as an opportunity to think very hard about a great alternative (I call it a *'Plan A$\alpha$'*), such that it will stand the test of time as a true and viable option, one that is likely to give you years of satisfaction and fulfillment.

In pursuing this tangible exercise, you will be buying yourself an insurance that may shield you from disappointment, just in case, if after putting in the hard work, you are unsuccessful in securing a position to join a residency training program. In developing a '*Plan Aα*', you often have to devote a significant amount of time and energy to explore what the alternative career path requires in terms of training and expense. You also need to evaluate it further to see if it will offer you the level of satisfaction that you are likely to obtain in the practice of medicine.

A simple exercise in developing a '*Plan Aα*' often begins with the simple question – What field would I have pursued if I did not pursue a career in medicine? The response to this question is a good beginning to a meaningful conversation, one that sometimes leads to a breakthrough, although not in the actual sense. A breakthrough in the sense that, a candidate may profess to not having ever considered the thought of an alternative career until that moment.

In the pages that follow, I will share with you the many options that I considered viable routes. Some are more direct than others in terms their possibilities, but every one of them can, with the right attitude and ingenuity meet one's life goals. While this book touches on the essentials of the select career paths, it is not as exhaustive companion book that provides you with all the information you will ever need. Additional information can be readily found on dedicated online channels and professional organizations' websites that cater to the specific needs of the profession. While some of the career options relate to the field of medicine, and are familiar professional routes to international medical graduates, others are tangential career paths, that may or may not really require the use of your medical background. Rather than separate the medical-related options from the non-medical ones, I have taken the liberty to discuss them in no set order.

In going through the pages that follow, take a moment after reading about each career option to imagine yourself in that profession. I think at this point, it is worthwhile to remind you that, in this day and age, the idea of a single career for a lifetime is becoming less of a reality. In other words, I would implore you to keep in mind that your next career move may not be your last one, but a foundation to pursue even greater ambition.

# ACKNOWLEDGEMENT

This book is dedicated to everyone in the profession who aspire to a life of fulfillment in the pursuit of their life goals.

## ♣ Clinical Fellowships

This career track is a viable option for international medical graduates, especially those who already have years of clinical experience, or have completed residency training in their home countries. Such positions are often based at tertiary hospitals that are already equipped to train residents and clinical fellows.

To obtain a clinical fellowship position often requires completion of the United States Medical Licensing Examinations, and obtaining ECFMG certification. In many instances, it require some years of experience in the field, not necessarily in the United States, and a strong letter of support from physicians familiar with the applicant's clinical skills. Some of these positions are available through the yearly clinical fellowship Match, while some are advertised as stand-alone programs. It is important to ascertain if the position is accredited by the Accreditation Council of Graduate Medical Education (ACGME), because not all clinical fellowship programs are accredited.

While getting into an accredited clinical fellowship position is the preferred route, it is sometimes advisable to accept a non-accredited positions as a way to get through the door, and build a good impression, in the hope to secure an offer of an accredited training program.

Many of these clinical fellowship programs last for two to three years. They are available across all specialties, although more common in the non-surgical fields. In select parts of the country, completing such a training especially at the top-tier institutions may lead to an opportunity to work as a clinician under the supervision of a senior faculty.

In select parts of the country, the combination of your ECFMG certification and completion of an accredited fellowship allows you to apply for a limited license during training, and after two to three years, may qualify you for a full license. With your full license, it is possible to secure a position that enables one to work in a clinical setting. Such opportunities often come with some degree of limitations in terms of clinical privileges. This may be so in surgical specialties, and in procedure-intensive areas where there are significant litigation and medical malpractice risks.

Such employment opportunities as described in the last paragraph arise from time to time in specialties where there is scarcity of clinical providers, and in underserved areas of the country that are less attractive to indigenous physicians.

## ♣ Non-Clinical Fellowships

While it is possible to obtain non-clinical fellowship positions with, or without having an ECFMG certification, having one has its benefit, and offers the chance to transition to a clinical fellowship when such opportunities occur. Many positions designated as non-clinical fellowships are in basic sciences, and usually involve non-clinical research. Contrary to what obtains in a clinical fellowship position, accepting a non-clinical fellowship position may mean that an individual may not be involved in the provision of direct clinical care.

Securing a non-clinical fellowship position may leads to further employment opportunities at research institutions, tertiary hospitals, and pharmaceutical companies. In these areas, there are ample opportunities for career progression, and the experience acquired can become transferable to managerial and leadership roles. In your role as a non-clinical researcher or assistant, you may find yourself working with accomplished faculties, and get opportunities to co-author publications in peer-reviewed journals. These esteemed faculties may also serve as mentors and advisors and propel your career even further in years to come.

While you really do not require additional post-MD degree to secure such positions, having an

MPH, MBA, or a PhD, is a valuable asset, especially if you are pursuing positions in top-tier hospitals. Even if your position does not require one, my advice is that you look for opportunities to study part-time for any postgraduate degree that aligns with your long term goals. This same reasoning applies to the need to pursue training opportunities to acquire additional skills related to your line of work. Many international medical graduates have followed this path at the beginning of their career.

## ♣ Nurse Anesthetist

While this professional path is not one that readily jumps out as an option, it is a recognized alternate career path. This is particularly so with international medical graduates who already have experience in the field, and who have strong desires to continue in their field. It is also an option for individual who desire to work in the field of anesthesiology, but are unable to secure an opportunity to pursue residency training in the field. Many institutions that offer this training program may require an applicant to complete additional training at a recognized nursing school, and acquire the necessary clinical experience before embarking on the two to three year training to become a nurse anesthetist.

While this aspect of nursing is very competitive, your educational background as a physician, and the additional certification of ECFMG makes you a desirable candidate. You are also likely to excel during training as an international medical graduate, since you already have prior clinical experience.

In many parts of the United States, these professionals are required to work under the supervision of a qualified anesthesiologist, although some states offer a greater degree of autonomy. A quick search over the internet will reveal a list of the various programs around the country. Becoming a nurse anesthetist is a viable career option that not only offers great compensation and opportunities for career growth, but also offers great flexibility in terms of work and family balance.

## ♣ Management Consulting

There seems to be ample opportunities in this field for candidates with a medical background. While many candidates tend to focus on the big consulting firms, there are several small and medium size firms that offer opportunities for employment. As an ECFMG-certified physician, not only are you able to apply your medical knowledge as a domain expert, you can also be a great assess when it comes to the problem-solving aspect of management. Medical graduates are often a great resource especially for projects that require people of diverse background and experience.

While it is possible to secure an entry-level job in this field without having completed additional postgraduate studies, having a post-MD degree in business administration, or business management may offer an added advantage. For those who find working in this field appealing, management consulting positions offer great opportunities for career advancement and income growth. For a candidate who is well motivated, as you advance in the field, experience acquired over the years can be applied in seeking senior positions in, and outside of the medical field.

## ♣ Nursing/Nurse Practitioner

Choosing a career path to become a nurse practitioner, is somewhat similar to that to become a nurse anesthetist, in that it requires you to undergo the required training to qualify as a registered nurse. It is after qualifying as a nurse and obtaining the necessary certification that one may then proceed to train as a nurse practitioner. This may be completed in a continuous manner, although some programs require a few months of practical clinical experience.

If you search the directory of nursing programs in the United States, select programs offer an accelerated track, and may consider your MD degree, with, or without your ECFMG certification into consideration in accepting you into training. In many cases, the years of training is limited to two or three years, after which you can apply for a full license to practice in any part of the country.

This career path not only allows you to stay in clinical medicine, it gives you the added flexibility to select a specialty that aligns with your interest, be it pediatrics, internal medicine, or psychiatry. In occasional instances, some international medical graduates have gone on to use the experience acquired in the practice of this profession to boost their competitiveness as a residency applicant.

While this is a possibility, my recommendation is that in choosing this career path, you should feel comfortable and be prepared to work as a nurse practitioner, and not make such a decision in the hope that the added qualification will boost your candidacy for residency application.

## ♣ Physician Assistant

This option of an alternative career path is a familiar one with many international graduates, although it is not always considered until many have been unsuccessful in obtaining a position for residency training. Training to become a physician assistant generally appeals to those who desire to work in surgical specialties, with many successfully obtaining positions in general surgery, orthopedics, neurosurgery and cardiothoracic surgery. As a physician assistant, you will be working under the supervision of a qualified physician. This career path is comparable to that of a nurse practitioner, although it is not often required that one qualify first as a nurse.

Individuals who choose this path may eventually find themselves after a few years of working in the field, as first-assistants during surgery, and may be granted limited surgical privileges. It is important to note that this career option is not limited only to those with interests in the surgical specialties, but can be a chosen track for an individual with a desire to work in non-surgical specialties.

As in the case of a nurse practitioner, your educational background as a physician, and the additional certification of ECFMG may offer you an added advantage in gaining admission and exceling in your studies. A career as a physician assistant can be a fulfilling career option, one that offers great compensation, opportunities for career growth in research and training. It is also a great career option in terms what it offers in terms of life-work flexibility and balance.

## ♣ Surgical Technician/Technologist

In considering this career option, it is important that you know the difference between training as a surgical technician and becoming a surgical assistant. This is further differentiated in the discussion outlined on the next page.

Training as a surgical technician may appeal to the international medical graduate with considerable financial constraints, and may serve as a spring board to gain an entry into a physician assistant training. It also an opportunity to get your feet through door and build relationships that may give you a chance to advance your career.

In select practices, especially in private settings, it is possible to earn a good income when you combine MD degree, ECFMG certification with your certification as a surgical technician, or technologist. This is likely in clinical settings where you are able perform managerial duties in the surgical department.

## ♣ Surgical Assistant

If your interest lies in the surgical field, becoming a surgical assistant and securing a position in a surgical specialty is one of the ways to go. This option is popular with those without adequate financial resources. In some cases, it may be a faster route to employment, even quicker than pursuing the surgical technician track. This is because as an ECFMG certified MD, some states offer a certification test, one that can be completed after the payment of a nominal fee, and one that most ECFMG certified MDs are successful. Although the certification route is gradually being modified to a format where a licensure based on an accrued number of practice hours.

Training to become a surgical assistant is less expensive when compared to the tuition cost to embark on a training as a surgical technologist. To train as a surgical assistant is also shorter, and for an ECFMG certified MD, in some parts of the country, it may be possible to get an exemption from some of the requirements to qualify as one.

Whereas, employment as a surgical technician abound all across the country with the opportunity of a reasonable income, that of a surgical assistant is less so, as it is hospital or practice-based, and are not as numerous as the former.

## ♣ Practice Administrator

Among the many paths chosen by international medical graduates who pursue postgraduate degrees – public health (MPH), health administration (MHA), or business administration (MBA), becoming a practice manager or administrator is not uncommon. As such positions are not always entry position, it may require that you work in a subordinate position for a reasonable period of time to build the necessary work experience, to fully qualify to function in such a capacity.

With so many practices and hospitals in need of professionals in this field, you prior clinical experience and the added value of a postgraduate degree tailored to the field opens the door of opportunity in this area. This career option may also become a gateway to becoming a health executive and to advance your career further. To excel in this field, it is important to build your professional network and to secure the guidance of those who are already established in the field.

## ♣ Practice Coordinator/Manager

This career option is a rather uncommon track, but the barrier to entry is not as high and may serve as a training ground in your journey to become a health executive. This field will only appeal to you if you are interested in the managerial, or operational aspects of healthcare. To secure such positions sometimes require that you have prior exposure to the operations of a medical practice, and this could be in the form of an internship as part of a postgraduate studies – MPH or MHA, or a self-initiated effort on your path. Where opportunities to intern do not exist, you can always apply to junior positions as associate. This will enable you to acquire necessary experience, and then advance to the position you really desire.

Once you attain your goal, do not settle at this level, instead, use the opportunity to build your skills, and establish a professional network that will serve in years to come. This career path is a viable route with a potential to advance to senior positions in management and operations.

## ♣ Research Coordinator

This is a popular path for many who in the course of preparing to apply for residency training, have completed additional post-graduate studies in fields like public health, biostatistics, or data science. As many of these study programs come with opportunities for internship, or practical training in the field, it has become a familiar route for many individuals.

Many of these positions are based in research departments of hospitals and research facilities. For those who are interested in clinical or non-clinical research, it can be a fulfilling career choice, with opportunities to contribute to the field of medicine without actually engaging in clinical practice. Working in such positions mean that you have opportunities to co-author publications in peer-reviewed journals.

In my experience, many candidates in the field have not chosen this track by design, instead, they selected such positions as a step to improve their credentials as they apply for residency positions. For those who plan to make a career out of this track, it is vital that you pursue your careers at institutions that offer opportunities for career advancement.

## ♣ Quality Assurance Associate

Popular among those with post-MD graduate training in public health is the field of quality assurance. These positions are in clinical settings, and require that you participate in quality control issues pertaining to the delivery of care. This position allows you to work closely with clinical providers, as you are involved in the day to day activities that has to do with the improvement of care delivery and, or utilization of resources.

As in the case of a career as a research coordinator, it is important that you think through this choice as a career path, and make sure it is a choice that will offer you fulfillment in years to come. This is relevant as you will find yourself working along colleagues whose role is to direct clinical care.

## ♣ Pharmaceutical - Sales

The next few pages of this book will be devoted to the various opportunities that exist in the pharmaceutical field. There is a significant overlap between the medical and pharmaceutical fields that makes it an attractive career option for medical graduates in general. In terms of remuneration, job satisfaction and fulfillment, pharmaceuticals in general is a popular career track for medical graduated.

Pharmaceutical sales is one of the many options that exist in this field. While sales may not be your cup of tea, it is one way to get into the field and begin to build your credentials. Once you are in the field, your experience will start to become relevant, and your relationships may open doors to greater opportunities. With so many pharmaceutical companies setting up around new innovations, the filed continues to expand. It is a field that offers many play their part in advancing the science.

## ♣ Pharmaceutical – Clinical Trials

This is one of the specialties that you will come across in the field of pharmaceuticals. Unlike pharmaceutical sales, the requirement for entry is a little different. This field is often a good fit for international medical graduates in general, with an MD degree with, or without an ECFMG certification. Since you will be engaged in some sort of scientific studies, a postgraduate degree in epidemiology, or related subjects will be helpful in this specialty.

In addition to the skills that relate directly to the work itself, you are likely to acquire people skills as you work teams, and collaborate with individuals in other units in your company. These skills are transferrable to other areas within, or outside the industry, especially if you decide to make further career changes.

## ♣ Pharmaceutical – Compliance/Safety

This specialty of pharmaceuticals is an ever expanding field, and one that offers opportunities for candidates with a medical background. Compliance and safety are critical aspects of the pharmaceutical industry. It is a specialty that will continue to demand the expertise of capable individuals. If you have concerns about how you will fit into such positions, many of these companies have entry-level position, and almost all of them offer adequate training in the field. This industry is well known for its ability to organize and sponsor conferences and seminars, so you are likely to get ample opportunities to develop quickly in the field.

## ♣ Pharmaceutical - Pharmacovigilance

There is significant overlap between pharmacovigilance and pharmaceutical safety as career options. The emphasis is on risk identification and surveillance. The overlap identified in some of these specialties is an added advantage, as this further opens up opportunities for career development for motivated candidates. In terms of developing a successful career in this specialty, you can also apply many of the same principles that were highlighted earlier in this book.

In terms of the requirements to begin a career in this field, it is similar to what was described for pharmaceutical safety positions. You may also stand a better chance in this field if you start out in another specialty, and use the experience and knowledge acquired to pursue a career in pharmacovigilance.

## ♣ Pharmaceutical – Non-Clinical Scientist

For the individual whose interest is research, pharmaceuticals is an area that can be considered, and one that may offer the same degree of satisfaction when compared to similar work in a tertiary hospital, or a research institution. If you are not ECFMG-certified, your options may be limited to this track, and you may not have direct contact with patients. This is contrary to the career option discussed on the next page.

In addition to the various pharmaceutical career options discussed so far, there are other less known career options that are too numerous to list in this book, but cannot be totally ignored. I will advise that you spend some time on a few of the popular job recruitment sites to see what positions are available and check their requirements in terms of experience and qualifications.

## ♣ Pharmaceutical – Clinical Scientist

Having an ECFMG certification offers you
the added advantage that you may, under
supervision, be able to work in clinical settings.
While there is a significant amount of opportunities
as a non-clinical scientist, this alternative may
appeal to individuals who have a strong attraction
to clinical work.

Even when such a position is not available,
remember that you can enter the field as a non-
scientist, and once you acquire the necessary skills
and experience, you can transition to the position of
a clinical scientist.

## ♣ Public Health – Research/Audit

Every state in the United States has a public health department that plays a critical role in the health and safety of the community. Every year, there are ample opportunities for individuals with a background in epidemiology and public health to apply to one of these positions. This career path often offers a stable work environment and a competitive income structure. This career option does to apply to everyone, but for those who are committed to a career in public health.

Available positions are often advertised on respective state government web sites.

## ♣ Medical Billing Consultant

This field offers opportunities for candidates with a medical background to serve in a senior positions in the billing departments of hospitals and private facilities. Working in this field will require completion of required medical billing and coding classes. Such courses usually last less than a year, with many available in an online format. This field also offers opportunity for those with entrepreneurial flair to establish independent billing companies.

An alternative approach to following a career in this track is to secure an entry-level position, while further training and necessary certifications are completed.

## ♣ Analyst – Investment Research

40

This a field that may not be familiar to many. It is a field that takes the individual outside of the comfort zone of medically related fields. Working in this field is no different from some of the none-medical fields mentioned in the early parts of this book. To work in this field, you may have to enroll in a short professional training and obtain the required certification to function in this field.

As an ECFMG-certified physician, you may find opportunities to work in this capacity by providing focus on medical and pharmaceutical companies. For a candidate who is well motivated, there is an opportunity to advance in the field and build a fulfilling career.

## ♣ Medical Journalism

While this career path is not a popular option for many international medical graduates. For those who have a genuine interest in the field, it is worth considering. Even though you may find yourself competing with others in this field, having a MD diploma is a tangible asset. A short-duration study course in journalism, or even a Master's degree in journalism may be advisable if this is a path that you desire to pursue.

## ♣ Writer/Author – Fiction/Non-Fiction

This is a viable option, although it is one with a less predictable path. It is less predictable in the sense that it takes a fair amount of effort and dedication to develop a career based solely on writing. In many cases, aspiring writers hone their skills while working in an unrelated area of work, or in a regular position until they make a success of the career. Even if you do not make of this choice of career early in the process, I encourage you not to give up as your best work tend to manifest as you build up experience about life and around your desire to write.

It is a career path that applies to individuals who are genuinely interested in writing. It is also helpful to keep in mind that there is a broad range of opportunities to write, from fiction to non-fiction, to children books and illustrations. The barrier often faced by many include the difficulty with getting a literary agent to represent your work. This is becoming less of an issue nowadays as you may elect to self-publish your work. Going this route means that you will be responsible for marketing and promoting your published books. In return, you get to keep a bigger proportion of the royalty due to you, while at the same time have sole ownership of your intellectual asset. In terms of career development, it is helpful to seeks opportunities to meet other writers, and if you can afford it, embark on a postgraduate Masters in Creative Writing.

## ♣ Non-Profit

In the non-profit arena are entities whose work centers around healthcare and disease prevention. Such entities have constant need for skills relating to project management, planning and implementation. While you may not be directly involved in the provision of clinical care, you may have an impact in forming policies that in turn shape the lives of many who are far remote from you.

Rather than limit their options to non-profit that is related to healthcare, some individuals have made a switch entirely outside of the realm of medicine, and work for other institutions. While it is a major change for many, you will discover that you will be using the same set of life and organizational skills as would in running a health-related non-profit organizations. In this filed, over the course of many years, it is not uncommon to see individuals rise up the rank to become an executive in the field.

## ♣ Clergy/Ministry

I have a few professional colleagues who have pursued this path soon after completing their medication, either in combination with the practice of medicine, or independently. For those who have a sense of calling to serve in this field, it is worth considering, and many who chose this path have gone on to have fulfilling careers. Opting for a career in religious ministry is a decision that is not for everyone, but one that is driven by a deep conviction and belief.

## ♣ Medical Sales Representative

A career as a medical sales representative is somewhat similar to that of individuals who are involved in pharmaceutical sales. While working as a pharmaceutical sales representative has the professional focusing on the sales of medications, a medical sales representative are engaged in the selling of a wide variety of items utilized in the treatment of patients.

Many of these items are broadly described as medical devices, such as catheterization stents used in cardiology, vascular grafts and related products utilized during vascular surgeries, and joint prosthesis and fixation hardware. This field often requires in-house training, and may fit individuals with compatible personal traits. There is no doubt that a career in this field can be a rewarding career, but you have to be prepared to engage in fair amount of travel and to work some unfavorable hours. In this choice of a career, you also have great opportunities to work for different companies, selling different products. Some, after many years, are able to establish as a medical distributor.

## ♣ Financial Planner

This is a career that is outside of the realm of healthcare, but one that many in the healthcare profession have a need of. In developing a career in this field, you may find yourself having a relative advantage over your peers in the field, as you are able to relate to medical professionals and maybe turn that access to opportunities to build a successful financial planning career.

Working in this filed often require specialized training, some of which will be provided, or sponsored once you gain an entry position in the field. In addition to the training that goes on while you are working, there are certifications that you will need to acquire for you to advance your career in the field.

## ♣ Investment Analyst

A career as an investment analyst is not one to draw the attention of international medical graduates as it is outside of the realms of clinical medicine. Many however have followed this path to building a successful career. It is often the case that awareness of the field follows a stint at business or management schools, but some based on an introduction by those who already work in the field have pursued this track as a career of choice.

There are often opportunities to begin at an entry level, and structured training sessions towards the necessary certification to be able to practice in the field. Some may have the choice to be a specialist as an investor in healthcare related business, or you may trained as a generalist to speculate across the industry as a generalist. As the work is often based on productivity, the remuneration is often great, with the added option of a performance bonus.

## ♣ Technology – Digital Health

There are many aspects to this field, one that constantly expanding and evolving to include everything to do with the delivery of healthcare to monitoring of patients. Despite not having a background in technology, there are opportunities to develop a career in this field. Your medical background makes you a desirable member of any design team, as your skills will be relevant when the final product is ready for testing and clinical trial. A good to start with exploring this field is to research the companies in this field, especially new companies that may have entry-level openings.

## ♣ Start-Up/Entrepreneurship

The entrepreneurial route is not a readily attractive option to many international medical graduates, since they are not that familiar with local terrain, and more not have a reasonable network to make a success of a such a career in a foreign country. There have been instances though, of individuals who while undergoing postgraduate studies have been successful in starting a business, either alone, or with fellow students.

While this choice is a viable one, it is a career path that you must pursue with care and with an awareness of the potential risk involved. It is definitely not a route for the risk-averse, but for those who have what it takes, it is a worthwhile choice, and one that may in the future yield in multiple folds.

## ♣ Medical Education

Many international medical graduates have found opportunities in pursuing the path of medical education as a career option, and becoming educators in the field. Some of these opportunities are available in the non-clinical subjects and basic sciences, often found in colleges' pre-med and basic science department.

Others have found opportunities to pursue a career in medical education teaching clinical subjects, working along with practicing clinicians, and helping to formulate study curriculum and play other supporting roles. In selecting this path as a choice of career, you must have an interest in teaching and truly believe that you will achieve satisfaction in helping others acquire knowledge. You may have to enroll in additional postgraduate courses in your chosen subject in order to advance further in the field.

## ♣ Advocacy

In your profession as medical professional, you are already familiar with this role, and must have been engaged in a significant amount of advocacy work in the course of your work, especially in relation to patients' care. To turn this into a primary vocation should not be so difficult, although it will require a fair amount of thinking and inventiveness on your part. There are definitely many organizations that are involved in advocacy work, both in healthcare and non-related fields. Many have political affiliations, and some are connected to charitable organizations.

The field of advocacy is often overlooked, but it is one field where your medical education can definitely be put into play. Developing a career in this field will require a significant commitment on your part, as it is a field where success is defined by your passion for the work and a desire to make a positive impact.

## ♣ Charity

Many healthcare workers engage in charitable work at one time, or the other in the course of their career. Not many medical graduates consider it a career option in the early stages of their career. Pursuing a career in this field does not mean you work as a volunteer, it means that you are paid to work as part of a team of experts who are devoted to a cause. In many case, these organizations will relate to healthcare, but nothing stops you from seeking opportunities outside of healthcare if you truly believe you can make an impact.

Your medical education is enough of a requirement to begin a career in this field. There are various aspects of non-profit work for those who elect to follow this path to choose from, including field work, policy design, project management and administration. In pursuing this career track, it is important that you become familiar with the field by attending relevant conferences, and where necessary use a career advisor, or a professional recruiter to develop your credentials for the non-profit industry.

## ♣ Advisory Services

If you to look around you, you will observe the many institutes spread all over the country. They consist of experts from various walks of life who are engaged in policy designs and analysis of political and economic trends. Many are described as think-tanks, and are involved in as many subjects as you can think about. Many policy changes that are implemented all over the world take their roots at some of these institutes.

It is a very interesting field, one that may allow you to make an impact without your involvement in direct clinical care. While you may not immediately qualify to play a role in a senior capacity, you will definitely qualify as a junior associate. You will be surprised how invaluable your medical education and your international experience is carving out a path for yourself in this area.

If this is a field that you are unfamiliar with, a good starting point is to secure internship opportunities in your area of interest. As mentioned earlier, this does not have to be limited to the healthcare field. What is important is to seek out practices that are engaged in the kind of work that you really connect with. With such a mindset, you will be surprised how quickly your passion for the work will drive your progress in the field.

## ♣ Medical Esthetics

Medical esthetics is a field where there are so many participants, and one that allows many to develop successful careers. While many have the image of the plastic surgeon engaged in reconstruction surgery in mind, the vast majority of those who work in the field have no medical degrees. The professionals involved in the field range from the technicians that operates equipment used for hair removal, skin toning, fat reduction, and varicose veins removal, to the trained specialist who is involved in procedures like botulinum (Botox) injections, liposuction and injection of facial dermal fillers.

With the abundance of certification courses on the subjects spread all over the country, you can easily register for the required courses to broaden your knowledge. You may need to become familiar with the state requirement in terms of setting up and registering as an estheticians. If you are really interested in developing expertise in the field and be able perform some of the procedures highlighted earlier, you can join an existing practice run by a family physician who specializes in such procedures.

Another route, for those who seek independence of practice, is to a nursing, or nursing practitioner degree, and use the certification to set up a practice. Whatever rout you pursue, over a short period of time, you will become familiar of the various possibilities in this field.

## ♣ Diet/Nutrition Consultant

In a field that is fairly open and has a lot of practitioners, there are opportunities to carve out a niche for international medical graduates with a desire to explore other alternatives. In its simplest form, you may opt to use your education to seek work opportunities in wellness and work as a counsellor. For those who really want to go deeper in the field, additional study leading to a diploma in nutrition, or related studies may allow to develop a practice that allows you to grow your own clientele. If this is a field that you are interested in, make an effort to complete additional research of the field and the requirements peculiar to your state of residence. You may also visit a local clinic to make direct observations and inquire about the career prospects from those who are already in the field.

## ♣ Marketing Associate

In discussing this career track as an option, my intention is to have you the reader, think outside of the usual domain for career transition. This is a very exciting field, one with many opportunities, and one that some can easily transition into as a choice of career. It often requires the completion of additional training in the field, either a Master's degree, or a diploma. Once you complete the required training, you may find yourself in a totally different world. You can then use your experience to seek out positions in fields relating to health and wellness tapping into your medical background, you may also elect to pursue a career in a field totally outside of the primary profession of medicine. There are professional organizations specific to the field which offer additional information on opportunities for training and mentoring.

## ♣ Medical Editor/Writer

This career option explores a field that may appeal to individuals who are interested in a career in publishing or medical writing. This is a select field that has gained prominence in recent years. It is similar to medical journalism in a way if your career leads you to work for a medical publication. It is different from medical journalism if your career leads you to provide industry-specific materials for a third party. While you will require an introduction to the field and guidance in pursuing this track, I am not aware of the need for any postgraduate study to prepare you for the field.

## ♣ Regulatory Officer

For those who have no reservation in working for government agencies, pharmaceutical and medical device companies, there are many opportunities to work in this field. There are organizations at both the state and federal level that are engaged in this field. There are also companies that require experts in this field as they navigate the process to introduce their drugs or medical devices into the market.

Training is often provided before entry into such positions, and ongoing once you begin your career. There are ample opportunities for career advancement once you start working in the field.. It is possible to use the experience acquired in the field to transfer from government agencies to private industries where senior level opportunities are likely to be advertised. While such a track is not designed for everyone, you will learn a lot once you begin to research the field.

## ♣ Health + Wellness Specialist

This career option is not a traditional track but one that may appeal to someone who is very interested in the subject of health and wellness. It may involve securing positions in the field as an associate to gain an understanding of the field. It is a constantly growing enterprise, with opportunities for those who are motivated to explore this option.

Over time, it is possible to either develop a career path in management, or if you like to be hands-on in the field, establish your own independent entity, or secure a franchise of your own. You will find your background in medicine helpful as you develop in this field.

## ♣ Software Engineering

Opting for a career in this field often means going back to school to learn more about the subject. Many such courses are in the form of condensed Master's program, but depending on how deep you want to go into the field, you may have to complete undergraduate program to better prepare them for a career in the field. Your background in medicine means that at the end of your training, you will a choice of opportunities of which areas to explore when you decide to join the work force.

## ♣ Electronic Health Career

With the advancement in clinical documentation and electronic health record, this field offers opportunities for individuals with medical backgrounds to play senior roles and become experts in the field. Many medical graduates begin their career in junior roles, and over time become trainers, specialists or consultants, and senior executives in the field. Your background in medicine definitely offers you an advantage.

## ♣ Medical Informatics/Manager

An interest in this field means going back to school to learn more about the subject. A number of colleges offer training programs in the form of a Master's program. Finding work that pays well after graduation is not that difficult, although you may have to start as a junior associate.

Your background in medicine often means that your progression in the field will be faster than your peers if you put your heart to it. You will also find out that at the end of your training, you have far more opportunities compared to your peers.

## ♣ Medical Devices

There are quite a number of companies involved in the manufacture and distribution of medical devices. Many of them often have roles for those with a medical background, outside of sales and marketing. They often have positions in areas like quality control, regulatory control, medical testing and product trial. Some also have positions to do with liaison with physician-users, and sometimes with the end-users – patients.

It is important that you have your resume structured to fit the job you have in mind, and to become familiar with basic requirements of positions in the field. Your medical background is of great value and makes unique as an applicant. A good starting point is to carefully looking through the job postings of the many companies in this field. Attending conferences also brings you closer to prospective employers. In some cases, you may have to use a professional recruiter to improve your chance of success.

## ♣ Medical Paralegal

This is a great starting point to get into the field of medical law, or medicolegal work. Not only is it a good entry point into the field, it is relatively inexpensive when compared to going straight to law school. It also allows you to get a taste of the field, and decide if it is a career meant for you. It is quite possible to secure work in an attorney's office as a paralegal, and start to build experience and develop a work profile in the field. Depending on your plan, you can proceed to complete the requirements to become a certified paralegal, and in the future pursue a career as an attorney.

While it is possible to end up in a law practice that rewards you well as a paralegal with an MD degree, I often advise that you don't stop there, but proceed to study part-time, or full-time for your law degree, and become licensed in your state of choice. I have come across individuals who have successfully followed this path. You can begin by doing a search of the law firms in your area, then search for programs that enable you to complete professional certification as a paralegal, and then take it from there.

## ♣ Legal Practitioner/Attorney

Pursuing a degree in law is a worthwhile career track. As explained earlier, some individuals get to this stage after working for some time as a paralegal, a preferred option for many at the beginning due to financial constraints. Some follow a direct path and attend classes to obtain a law degree. Your MD degree has an inherent value at the time you elect to begin the practice of law, although it is not compulsory that you practice in the medicolegal field.

## ♣ Real Estate Broker

This career option rarely crosses the mind of individuals with a medical background in the early stages of their career. Here, were are talking about it as one of the alternatives to consider if getting into a residency program has not gone according to plan. The good thing about this field is that you can study for the license to become a real estate broker part-time while holding down another job. You can also do the work part-time while you develop skills in other areas. As someone with a medical background, it may be an advantage if you have easy access to clients in the medical field who can afford high-value homes. You may also use this initial experience to pursue a career in real estate law. You never know which door will open in pursuing this career track.

A simple search in your local community will reveal available real estate broker training classes, as well as a directory of real estate firms. You can make a stop at local real estate brokerage offices talk to professional who are already in the field.

## ♣ Teaching Career

There are instances of individuals changing from a career in medicine to teaching elementary school children to fulfill the desire to teach. References to such professionals are not isolated events, and the world is full of stories of individuals who have made a complete switch from one profession to the other. For many with a medical background, the switch does not need to be of the same degree, and may take the form of teaching basic sciences at a medical school, or at a preparatory outfit for individuals preparing to attend medical school.

For those who truly see a career in teaching as a calling, you definitely will need to complete the training in the field, and obtain the necessary certification to embark on such a career. A certificate, a diploma, or a Master's degree are options available to pursue in preparation for entry into the field. It is definitely a worthy career to explore.

## ♣ Information Technology Officer

Pursuing a career in this field often means taking the time to embark on a course of study to become proficient in the field. Available courses are in the form of Master's program, often last from one to two years. Your background in medicine also means that at the end of your training, you will have a choice of opportunities on where to apply your skills in the work force.

## ♣ Human Resources Manager

This is another non-traditional career track for someone who had gone through the pain of completing medical school education. Human resource professionals rank high among highly paid professions, especially at moderate and large size companies. Many of us are familiar with human resource professionals every time we start a new job, or inquire about one. The larger the organization, the bigger the human resource department of an organization. Senior professionals in the field often exert great influence during recruitment process, and some become senior executives that influence the direction of their organizations.

Pursing a Master's degree with a concentration in human resource management will provide you with the required qualifications to enter the industry. As you gain a better understanding of the field, you can then prepare yourself to explore the various opportunities. It is also possible to pursue postgraduate studies in business administration with concentration on human resource management. It is a career that is worth researching further. While starting out in this field may not offer you a big income at the beginning, career progression is usually very promising.

## ♣ Professional Recruitment

This choice of career is somewhat related to a career as a human resource personnel. In this choice of profession, you will find yourself playing an active role between the human resource personnel and prospective job seekers. It is an exciting career choice, where you may find yourself guiding the careers of others and presenting them to prospective employers. In some cases, individuals who pursue this career, start out as a human resource personnel, and slowly work their way up the ladder.

A postgraduate degree in the field often establishes you as someone with a keen  interest in the field, although it should not be viewed as a barrier to entry.

## ♣ Business Analyst

With many international graduates pursuing additional studies in business management and administration, a career as a business analyst is a viable option. Do not be discouraged if you find yourself competing with graduates who had pursued business studies as undergraduates. For individuals who take the time to develop their credentials and make it relevant to the field, it is quite possible to pursue a career opportunities in the field.

## ♣ Psychotherapist

For individuals who are committed to this field, and are unable to secure residency positions in psychiatry or any other medical fields, training as a psychotherapist may appeal to those who are drawn to the field and believe it will offer them a reasonable degree of level of satisfaction and fulfilment.

Advanced training is often required to qualify to practice in this field, with many universities offering courses as both full-time and part-time. In many instances, once you are qualified as a psychotherapist, and have a state license, you may be able to set up an independent practice to better serve your patient population.

# ABOUT THE AUTHOR

Olarewaju Oladipo is the founder of KAINJI, a career mentoring and networking platform with a focus on the needs of Nigerian medical graduates in pursuit of career in the United States.

This initiative has not only triggered a culture shift in the attitudes of young professionals of Nigerian descent (and others), it has eased the challenges that many international medical professionals face when they arrive in the United States. The platform remains active and continues to offer the necessary guidance that is so important in the early, critical stages of the careers of international medical graduates.

Since its inception many years ago, KAINJI has grown to be a grassroot community of individuals who are committed to sharing their knowledge and supporting one another and the community at large – both in the United States and in Nigeria.

For additional information on this book, seminars, individually tailored mentoring and tutoring on USMLE preparation and guidance on the process of applying for residency training program for the international graduate, visit our website www.kainji.org

MORE ABOUT THE AUTHOR

Olarewaju Oladipo is an author (fiction and non-fiction)
whose writing career began while practicing as an
orthopedic surgeon. Following the release of his earlier
books "The White Coat" (2006) and "House Calls"
(2007), he dedicated the next few years to crafting
motivational quotes written using the Twitter handle
@3SqMeals as Dr. O' and publishing multiple books
under the '3SqMeals Tweets – Not Your Typical Meal'
series.

His works of fiction include the "North Main Street"
mystery series and the "Once A Doc" medical fiction
series, with the release of Barber's Haven (2015), 'A
Patient called Emma' (2015) and 'Ghost Bus (2016).

'The Sculpture Garden' series is based on actual
sculptures and part of an ongoing effort to support the
work of local artists in Nigeria, fund the establishment
of sustainable sculpture gardens, and sponsor worldwide
collaborations with art institutions.

Two Blind Men (2017) was the first of a collection of
short stories of the 'Sculpture Garden' series. Tortoise
of Many Colors (2017), The Tree of Wonder (2017), and
Esther (2018) are other books in the series.

Medical Residency Guide for the International Medical
Graduates – What You Need To Know Before You
Apply (2015) is part of the ongoing series geared
towards the specific needs of international medical
graduates, especially those emigrating from Nigeria.

---

All books are available in paperbacks and ebook formats on Amazon, Kobo, Smashwords, and on author's website (www.olarewajuoladipo.com) and blog (www.olarewajuoladipo.org ).

www.ingramcontent.com/pod-product-compliance
Lightning Source LLC
Chambersburg PA
CBHW031152250726

48655CB00002B/944